BALD EAGLE
LIFE LESSONS

Based on the True Story Of a Bald Eagle Nest

Volume 1

DARRYL ZOLLER

To Jim,
With Thanks!
Darryl

PRESS

Bald Eagle Life Lessons
Based on the True Story Of a Bald Eagle Nest Volume 1
by Darryl Zoller

Printed in the United States of America.

ISBN 9781498471374

Unless otherwise indicated, Scripture quotations are from The Holy Bible, New International Version® Copyright ©1973, 1978, 1984 by International Bible Society.

www.xulonpress.com

TABLE OF CONTENTS

To my mother,
Betty Giles Zoller,
who gave me roots and wings.

ACKNOWLEDGMENTS

Special thanks to

Christine Zoller, my wife, Jim Hall, my Editor, and Pennsylvania Game Commission and Travis Lau for the courtesy of the images from the live stream feed cameras and permission to use the photographs I've taken of the nest in this book.

INTRODUCTION

Two winters ago, the Pennsylvania Game Commission arranged for the installation of a high definition camera at a bald eagle nest near our home in south central Pennsylvania.

This camera provides a live stream video feed to the public on the internet. I began watching in January, 2015 and continued watching the eagles, eggs, and eaglets until the eaglets fledged (took their first flight) in June of 2015, when the nesting season was complete.

I used my digital camera to take still pictures of the nest images I saw on my computer screen. I had prints made of my best photographs.

As the nesting seasons developed, I saw differences and similarities between bald eagle life and human life. As an ordained church pastor. I began noticing connections between how the bald eagles live and Christian faith, life, and relationships.

My knowledge base flows from thousands of hours spent in direct observation of the nests and from reading general interest information about the life of eagles published online by the Pennsylvania Game Commission.

It came to me that the bald eagle story and its connections to our faith, life, and relationships needed to be shared in photographs and words. I carefully selected sixteen representative photographs of bald eagle life and I went to work writing about each one. Once I had chosen the photos to use in this book, the words about them flowed from me like a stream. It was a joy to write about how bald eagles live and what life lessons God might be revealing from observing bald eagle family life, including the Christian marriage covenant.

Enjoy the bald eagle life photos and the life lessons that God might be teaching us. I pray that you might reflect on them. Discover what bald eagles have to teach us about ourselves, our relation to each other, and to God.

April 4, 2016

The thoughts expressed in this book are my own. They do not necessarily represent those of the Pennsylvania Game Commission or its partners.

BEAK

How do bald eagles build a nest? How do they lay eggs? Raise eaglets? Teach them to fly? Thanks to cameras placed by Pennsylvania Game Commission at a bald eagle nest in south central Pennsylvania, millions of viewers have thrilled to discover the answers to these questions and more. Only recently have we had the privilege of being eyewitnesses to the nesting season of North America's native eagle—the bald eagle.

As I watched the nest near me during the past two nesting seasons, I marveled at these majestic birds, the bald eagles, created by God, our loving heavenly Father. As eagles prepare a nest, lay eggs, raise their eaglets, and teach them to fly, we see that God may be teaching us valuable life lessons.

At the start of a nesting season, there are two adult eagles, one male and one female, each one already at least five years old, who are now able to produce offspring. Before the nesting season, they first noticed and became attracted to each other. Then began a courtship which included breath taking aerobatics in which they clasp each other's feet.

The photo above shows another courtship behavior—the beak touch, which I often saw when they were at the nest. The beak touch is a sign of affection between a mated pair of adult bald eagles. There is a life lesson that we can learn from the bald eagle's "kiss" – the beak touch. The beak touch is given between a male and female bald eagle in a committed, lifelong relationship.

I met my future wife in the first semester of college and immediately felt attracted to her. After a few dates, we began to fall in love and had our first kiss. Five years of courtship followed. At last we were ready to make our covenant of Christian marriage. At the seminary chapel, we exchanged vows and rings and had our first kiss as husband and wife. Forty-two years later, we exchange at least one meaningful kiss once (or more) a day!

The life lesson from the eagles is clear. For a healthy, vibrant relationship, show affection daily. Keep the fire of your love for each other burning bright.

Nest

This photo, above, shows the bald eagle pair at the nest. To prepare for having offspring, the eagles need a nest. If they don't already have one, they build a new nest.

They look for a tall tree with a large fork in the trunk, where a nest may be securely seated. Then they build their nest of sticks and grasses, with the sticks forming the outer framework.

The grasses inside the sticks serve as soft bedding for the eggs or nestlings. The pair will use their nest for season after season. Understand that the nest is a nursery for their young, not a bedroom for the adults! Adult eagles roost on tree branches at night. They sleep standing up, gripping a tree branch with their feet.

God has taught the bald eagles how to improvise. The fork in the tree, the sticks, and the grasses combine to provide safety and peace for the eagles' offspring. The bald eagle lesson is to use what's easily found to provide a safe and comfortable place for the young.

When my wife was a newborn, her parents, did not yet own a crib, so they used a bureau drawer! They laid their firstborn daughter in the drawer whenever she needed a nap or sleep. Perhaps the life lesson in our materialistic culture is that God is teaching us to keep things simple. Look around you. God supplies our simple, basic needs!

STICKS

As you can see in my photo, above, the eagles work together to place sticks carefully of all sizes, then weave them together to make an outer wall. Sticks strengthen the nest and rise inches above the center grasses, much like the side-rails we might see at a baby's crib.

God has shown the eagles that a stick wall is necessary to raise their young, to keep intruders out and the chicks in. The eagles teach us that it's good to have healthy boundaries for our own children. The Lord being our helper, the life lesson is that we need to keep what's harmful out and keep our children safe in the "nest" we call home.

GRASSES

In the photo, above, an eagle is landing with a bundle of grasses for the nest. The nest's bed is made of these soft and comfortable grasses. Before eggs are laid, the parents dig a sloping, round hole called a bole a few inches deep. Once the eggs are laid, the eagles take turns nesting over the eggs, keeping the eggs warm and dry. The egg cup ensures the eggs are not broken by the weight of the eight to fourteen pound birds.

Over time, grasses break down and sticks eventually snap. The eagles are always working to maintain and improve the nest. The next generation is at stake. Although we do not use sticks and grass to make a home for our children and youth, we find that the eagles set a great example for us in parenting—firm but soft, strong and safe.

We only have our children for a few good years before they must "leave the nest," so with God's help, the life lesson is that we must strive to do our very best while they are in our care. Parenting is sacred work. If we will ask, God will give us help, strength, and wisdom, as we need it, in all that we do for our children and youth.

LEAVES

W hen I was watching a bald eagle nest in winter near me, I wondered how they were going to remove the snow. As you can see in the photo, they did not remove it. They just brought oak leaves – for new grasses off nest were still buried in snow – to cover it. This is the eagle's way. They have no snow shovel or snow blower. On their feet are talons, about as hard and thick as a dog's toenail. The talons are not meant to be used for clearing snow from a nest. The talons are for grasping fish or other game, so the "Plan B" God has taught the eagles is simply to cover the snow as described above.

The eagles have learned how to deal with the weather and its effects. Our Creator has equipped eagles to endure wind, rain, snow, and cold. God has given eagles a warm and comfortable coat of over 7,000 feathers. A snowfall only slows their work for a few hours. They know what to do and they do it. They build anew!

The eagles know that warmer days are ahead. Snows will eventually melt, leaving no trace. The eagles show us how to more fully trust that God is "making everything new!" (Revelation 21:5). Eagles just get back to work each day. In life we find there are many troubles which suddenly arise which cannot be cleared away immediately. A setback, though, is often simply a set*up* for a come*back*.

COOT

What foods do bald eagles like to eat? They eat mostly fish. Eagle eyesight is several times sharper than ours. They can spot a fish swimming in a lake from a mile away. They get all their energy and water from the foods they eat. Bald eagles are meat-eaters. Next to fish, they like small game such as squirrels, rabbits, opossum, turtles and even snakes. They can carry up to four pounds of food in one trip. If they catch a fish too heavy to lift, they stroke their wings to swim the fish to shore, where they can eat it until it is light enough to carry elsewhere.

In the photo, the eagle is eating an American Coot. The coot, an aquatic bird, lives on plant life found at the water's edge. Because the coot has a slow, stumbling take-off, eagles find it easy to swoop in and catch it, so they catch coot more often than any other bird. Eagles snatch their prey with their strong feet. The grip of eagles' feet is several times stronger than our handgrip! What's more, the wingspan of a bald eagle varies from 6 to 8 feet! The bald eagle is well-designed by God to catch its own food.

Bald eagles need eight to twenty-four ounces of meat per day to thrive. Jesus taught his followers to pray, "Give us this day our daily bread" (Matthew 6:11). Since our heavenly Father provides daily food for the eagles, how much more does He want to provide for our daily needs? Of course, this does not mean that we are to just sit idly by and wait for God to bring us food. The lesson is that we should trust in God to help us as we work for our daily needs to be met.

EGGS

E agle eggs are laid five to ten days after mating. They measure about two and three-quarters by two and one half inches. Their color is dull white and unmarked.

A brood patch is an area of skin—barren of feathers—underneath the eagles, both male and female. God has designed the brood patch so that the hot blood vessels under the skin keep the eggs at just the right temperature to develop and hatch after about thirty-five days.

The female bald eagle lays between one to four eggs. Typically there are two eggs. However many are laid, the number of eggs is called a clutch. After the first egg is laid, another one may be laid in two to three days.

God has designed the eagles to know how many minutes to intentionally expose the first egg to the cold winter air. That way the egg matures more slowly. The second egg can catch up to the first in its maturation. When both hatch, they hatch closer to each other in time and the two nestlings are more alike in size and weight at hatching. This permits the second-hatched eaglet a better chance to survive a sibling rivalry with the first-hatched chick.

Truly, bald eagles and their eggs are amazing creations of God! The Psalmist exclaimed "I praise you because I am fearfully and wonderfully made" (Psalm 139:14a).

Since God has let the eagles know it's important to defend their eggs and tenderly care for them, how much more should we agree with God to do the same for our own unborn children? The eagle lesson is to preserve and protect developing life.

TEAM

H ere is a photo of the eagles, above, facing the sunset. One is standing and the other is seated over the eggs. The mated pair works as a team to bring the eggs to hatching and the eaglets to fledging – taking their first flight. Eagles take turns covering the eggs and spending time off nest in search of food. When the eaglets are hatched, they will continue to work as a team, supplying the young with protection and food. They will even feed them, beak-to-beak. The nestlings will eat the same foods that the adults eat, small bits of fish, mammals, reptiles, or amphibians.

Whether it is building the nest, covering the eggs till they hatch, or feeding the eaglets until they are able to fly, the adult eagles are there for them, working as a team.

God has wired the DNA of the bald eagle pair to work as a team. The life lesson for committed couples today is to follow their example of teamwork.

TURN

In this photo, above, it is a sunny morning. The eagle in the back has just arrived. The eagle in front is getting ready to fly off. Eagles take turns at nesting over the eggs.

For the health of the eaglets developing inside the egg, the eagles cover the eggs, keeping them warm. When they rise off the eggs, they gently turn the eggs over, rolling them to ensure even temperatures inside.

Our God is with us always, so we need to be there for our own children, when they need us most. Solomon wisely observed "Train a child in the way he should go, and when he is old he will not turn from it" (Proverbs 22:6).

The eagle life lesson for us is obvious. We too need to take turns at minding our children as they grow. Spending special time with a youngster is a very good thing.

FLY

In the photo a bald eagle is lifting off the snowy nest to fly. The wings and tail are raised high. The eagle thrusts its whole body forward. To watch the eagles take off from the nest or to make a landing is a great thrill.

While off the nest, bald eagles soar! Spreading their mighty wings, they're able to take advantage of warm, upward air currents called thermals and then, with wings spread wide, glide effortlessly across the sky.

Bald eagles do not always take to the air to hunt for game like other raptors do. Instead, they perch on a high branch of a barren tree near their nest and look for easy prey. They may notice a fish swimming in a lake and swoop in to snatch it from the water with their strong feet and sharp talons. They may see a squirrel, snake, or turtle exposed in the open and descend to grasp it. God has taught eagles to be patient and watchful. When opportunities to catch game happen, eagles are ready to fly!

At the nest, the eagles often fly in with a bunch of grass or a sturdy stick to repair or improve the nest. God has taught them how to be great nest builders.

A favorite verse of Jews and Christians alike is Isaiah 40:31: "But those who hope in the Lord will renew their strength. They will soar on wings like eagles; they will run and not grow weary, they will walk and not be faint."

Bald eagles fly in and out of the nest. Higher and higher, they *soar*! Believers who hope in the Lord, who watch eagles soar, experience a God-given renewal of body, mind, and spirit. Since God has taught the eagles to soar, so God will also help us soar to new heights of hope and strength for daily living, if we will ask Him. Our Lord desires the highest and best for each one of us. Eagles give us hope, renewal, and strength, and they teach us patience and watchfulness. What wonderful gifts they give and what inspiring lessons they teach us!

CALL

F or such a majestic bird, the bald eagle has a shrill, high-pitched voice. An eagle's voice sounds like a squeaky cackle or laugh. There are three basic eagle calls: a peal, a loud call, and chatter. The eagles use calls to communicate with each other. For instance, when one eagle is on the nest and the other is off and it is time to switch, the nesting eagle will peal or call to summon its mate.

In the photo the eagle, head raised, is calling the mate to come and relieve him or her of nesting duty. Within seconds or minutes the mate will come to the nest. One eagle then stays to incubate the eggs and the other eagle is free to fly away for a break or to find and consume a meal.

Bald eagles also call – loudly – if an intruder threatens the nest. The loud call warns off the intruder and summons the eagle mate to come quickly.

We don't understand what all eagle calls mean, but we often see how the calls they make help them communicate with each other. For example, the chatter between the male and female eagles strengthens their relationship as a mated pair.

God has given eagles different calls to assist them in communicating. When an eagle's call is heard, it reminds us that God still calls us to listen to Him each day. Be listening for God's call, his unique voice in your life. God's voice may be a "gentle whisper" (1 Kings 19:12) showing you a godly choice to make or a specific direction in which to move.

The life lesson of the calling eagles is that we too need to listen and speak. God has given us ears to listen and mouths to speak. Let us hear and speak well to deepen our relationship with God and with each other.

SLEEP

After sunset, bald eagles normally roost in a tree for the night. Eagles sleep standing up, gripping a branch with their feet. The head is spun around to the back and ducked under a wing. How different they are from us! We prefer to sleep in a warm, dry, clean bed with a pillow under our head.

During the nesting season, when there are eggs or newly hatched eaglets, a parent eagle rests over the eggs or eaglets to keep them warm, help them sleep, and defend them from intruders. In the photo we see an eagle before dawn nesting over the eggs. It's fast asleep with its head back, ducked securely under a wing.

When morning breaks, there are a variety sounds to be heard from off nest. A rooster crows, for example, dogs bark, Canada geese honk, and songbirds raise melodies in praise of their Maker. Passing trains, planes, and automobiles add to the sounds at dawn. One wonders how the nesting eagle can sleep through this din of noises.

With the first rays of sunlight, the eagle awakens and resumes its watch. Within minutes, the eagle may call for its mate to come. Very soon after that, the off-nest eagle may arrive and trade places with the nesting eagle.

Waking or sleeping, the eagles are on duty, providing care to their young at the nest. The pattern of their lives reminds us of God's watchfulness over our own lives. The eagles set an example of faithfulness akin to God's. The lesson for eagle watchers is to rejoice in the knowledge that our heavenly Father is always watching over us.

GRIT

In this photo, the nesting eagle holds a vigil encased in a snowfall. Snow is even seen on its back feathers.

It takes grit – firmness of spirit – to stay over eggs after a snowfall. Eagles show courage and staying power!

Ever patient and persistent, bald eagles valiantly persevere. The apostle Paul faced many challenges to his missionary efforts, but asked the Christians in Rome, "Who shall separate us from the love of Christ? Shall trouble or hardship or persecution or famine or nakedness?" (Romans 8:35).

As believers, we rejoice in Paul's answer to his own question, "No, in all these things we are more than conquerors through him who loved us. For I am convinced that neither death nor life, neither angels nor demons, neither the present nor the future, nor any powers, neither height nor depth, nor anything else in all creation, will be able to separate us from the love of God that is in Christ Jesus our Lord" (Romans 8:37-39).

Come what may, we need to learn to be like the eagles – patient and steadfast in adversity. God has well-equipped and taught bald eagles to endure. "When the storms of life are raging" (Charles Albert Tindley), Our God, who keeps his promises, will never leave us or forsake us.

SPREAD

Whenever it rains, the nesting eagle spreads its wings to cover the eggs or eaglets, and nest. This photo shows another occasion for spreading its wings. A pesky squirrel has just come too close to the nest! The eagle has quickly spread its wings in defense of the nest.

The term "spread-eagle" originated in the sixteenth century, when it referred to the image of an eagle with wings and legs spread. An armorial ensign might feature a spread-eagle image.

In our time, with live video camera eagle nest views, we are amazed to see what a real spread-eagle looks like! The mighty wings are spread wide to cover a large area of the nest. Whether eagle wings cover the nest to protect it from rain, snow, or strong sunlight or to fend off a pesky squirrel, it is a vivid display of protection and defense of their nest.

There's a beautiful love story in the Old Testament about a woman named Ruth who loved her mother-in-law, Naomi. As a reward for her love and faithfulness to Naomi, a kinsman named Boaz said kindly to Ruth, "May the Lord repay you for what you have done. May you be richly rewarded by the Lord, the God of Israel, *under whose wings you have come to take refuge*" (Ruth 2:12).

Happily, Boaz and Ruth soon marry. The "rest of the story" is found in Matthew 1:5*b*-6*a*, '*Boaz* (became) *the father of Obed, whose mother was Ruth, Obed* (became) *the father of Jesse, and Jesse* (became) *the father of King David.*" In Luke 2:4, we pick up the genealogy: "So Joseph also went up from the town of Nazareth in Galilee to Judea, to Bethlehem, the town of David, *because he belonged to the house and line of David.*

The Bible is truly a love-letter from God. Like the spread-open wings of an eagle, the pages of a spread-open Bible reveal the love God has for the world. Jesus himself used the imagery of sheltering wings to express his longings for the people of Jerusalem. He said, "How often I have longed to gather your children together, as a hen gathers her chicks *under her wings*, but you were not willing" (Luke 13:34*b*).

The spiritual take-away from the spread-eagle pose is that God wants us to find the help we need under His wings, too. When Jesus was crucified on the Cross, his arms were outstretched. He said to all those gathered under him, "Father, forgive them" (Luke 23:34*a*). If you haven't already accepted Jesus Christ as your Savior, I pray you will take refuge eternally under the sheltering wings of his forgiveness and salvation.

TIME

In this photo we see an adult eagle leaning over the two eaglets, so new that they still sport the whitish-grey fuzzy down they had when they first emerged from their eggshells.

Small and weak at the moment of hatching, each chick weighs only as much as a stick of butter and is so tired from pecking its way out of the shell that it can't hold up its head! Growth, however, is extremely rapid. Feathers appear three to four weeks after hatching. By weeks six to seven the eaglets can walk. Three months after hatching, the eaglets can take their first flight. After that, the eaglets are called fledglings.

In the nest I watch in south central Pennsylvania, the bald eagle pair spends one to three months getting the nest ready for egg-laying. After eggs are laid, there are roughly thirty-five days of sitting over the eggs till the eaglets hatch. Then follows another three months of feeding and caring for the eaglets in the nest until they can fly. Gathering enough food to help them grow is a monumental task for the parents. Consider the season of summer as well, when the adults must continue to feed the fledglings for several more weeks until they can teach them to find their own food. Summer is also spent teaching the fledglings the art of flying. It's not until mid-autumn, that the fledglings are completely on their own.

From start to finish, the parental process of preparing the nest, laying eggs, incubating the eggs, feeding the growing eaglets, teaching them to fly and find their own food can add up to ten to eleven months of constant work. Bald eagles expend much time and effort to raise a nest of eaglets to independence.

The eagle life lesson is that, the Lord being our helper, great parenting takes considerable time and effort to yield the best possible result. God has equipped eagles to shine as bright lights as they exercise their parenting knowledge and skill. Our loving heavenly Father is eager to equip us to be great parents, too. As our children grow up, God delights in partnering with us to raise our young in every way that pleases him.

LOVE

This photo shows a mated pair of bald eagles gazing upon a brilliant sunset. Their eggs have not yet been laid and their nest is covered with snow. The eagles haven't had time yet to find and gather new bedding leaves and grasses for the top of the nest.

In our forty-two years of marriage, there have been countless sunsets that my wife and I have enjoyed seeing. The pastel colors on the far horizon are a glorious sight before dark. One could say that a sunset somehow displays the colors of true love, shared.

When they are five years old, bald eagles are sexually mature. They are soon attracted to each other and form mated pairs. Eagles show affection for each other by lingering looks, brushing against each other in the nest, and dozens of beak touches.

Bald eagles also show their love for each other by all the work they do – bringing sticks and grasses to the nest, nesting over the eggs, taking turns on and off the nest, bringing each other food when necessary, catching food to feed the eaglets for three months, bringing food to the fledglings for several more weeks after the eaglets have fledged, and teaching the fledglings how to fly and find their own food. The goal, of course, is to help their offspring achieve independence in the wild.

In the musical "Fiddler on the Roof," Tevye asks his wife, Golde, "Do you love me?" In response, Golde sings, "Do I love him? For twenty-five years I've lived with him, fought with him, starved with him. Twenty-five years, my bed is his..." Her final answer is, "I suppose I do."

Bald eagles mate for life. From year five of their life until either one dies, they are a mated pair, attracted and committed to each other. Is that love? Maybe not in the way we think of married love, but we would call it love. Unlike us, mated bald eagle pairs keep laying eggs and raising eaglets long after our human bodies won't yield any more children. Yes, eagles are fertile and able to have a new nest family every year, right up to the end of their lives – such is the strength which God has given them.

The life lesson God teaches us through the bald eagles is that their "love" is for a lifetime! The bald eagles are an excellent model of a committed relationship. They show us a love that lasts! If bald eagles, who are wild, can keep commitment alive, how much more God would have us, in covenantal marriage, to stay in love and committed to one another.

The next time you gaze at the colors God has painted across the horizon at sunset, trust that God's love for you is always there, whether you are married, single, young or old.

BIBLIOGRAPHY

Pennsylvania Game Commission. "Pennsylvania Bald Eagles." www.pgc.com. http://www.portal.state.pa.us/portal/server.pt?open=514&objID=1592549&mode=2 (Accessed April 2, 2016).

Pennsylvania Game Commission. Korber, Kathy and Doug Gross. "Bald Eagle Identification Tips." www.pgc.com. http://www.portal.state.pa.us/portal/server.pt?open=514&objID=1734395&mode=2 (Accessed April 2, 2016).

Pennsylvania Game Commission. "Bald Eagle Fast Facts." www.pgc.com. http://www.portal.state.pa.us/portal/server.pt?open=514&objID=1734410&mode=2 (Accessed April 2, 2016).

Pennsylvania Game Commission. "Bald Eagle Wildlife Note." www.pgc.com. http://www.portal.state.pa.us/portal/server.pt?open=514&objID=1748670&mode=2 (Accessed April 2, 2016).

Pennsylvania Game Commission. "Pennsylvania Bald Eagles: Celebrating 30 Years of Restoration" (Documentary). www.pgc.com. https://www.youtube.com/watch?v=-4DK0sCiMd8 (Accessed April 2, 2016)

Pennsylvania Game Commission. "Educator's Guide to Celebrating Pennsylvania Bald Eagles" (Downloadable Booklet: May, 2014). www.pgc.com. http://www.portal.state.pa.us/portal/server.pt/community/education/9110 (Accessed April 2, 2106).

ABOUT THE AUTHOR

Darryl Zoller first became interested in bald eagle life in 2015 while watching a live stream video feed – provided by the Pennsylvania Game Commission – of the bald eagle nest near where he lives in south central Pennsylvania.

Darryl, an ordained church pastor, is married to Christine. They raised three sons, all of whom have since "left the nest."

Darryl likes to hear from his readers and is available for speaking engagements by contacting him at: baldeaglelifelessons@gmail.com

CPSIA information can be obtained
at www.ICGtesting.com
Printed in the USA
BVOW07s0952210416

445069BV00004B/6/P

9 781498 471374